Resurrected!

Resurrected!

**The Historical Truth
of the Most Important Event
in Human History -
And Why It Matters**

(Second Edition)

Dr. John Morris

© 2017 Dr. John Morris. All rights reserved. No part of this book may be distributed, posted, or reproduced in any form or by any means without the prior written permission of the author.

Cover image © James Steidl/123rf.com. Used by permission. All rights reserved.

Unless otherwise indicated, all Scripture quotations are taken from the Holy Bible, New International Version® (NIV®) © 1973, 1978, 1984, 2011 by Biblica, Inc.® Used by permission. All rights reserved worldwide. New International Version® and NIV® are registered trademarks of Biblica, Inc. Use of either trademark for the offering of goods or services requires the prior written consent of Biblica US, Inc.

Additional Scripture quotations are taken from the Holy Bible, New Living Translation, © 1996, 2004, 2007, 2013, 2015 by Tyndale House Foundation. Used by permission of Tyndale House Publishers, Inc., Carol Stream, Illinois 60188. All rights reserved.

ISBN-13: 9781539649984
ISBN-10: 1539649989
Library of Congress Control Number: 2016917638
CreateSpace Independent Publishing Platform
North Charleston, South Carolina

Resurrected! The Historical Truth of the Most Important Event in Human History–And Why It Matters was first released in February 2016. By March 2016, it was a **#1 Best Seller** in Christian Books and eBooks for Easter and Lent on Amazon.com. Here are some of the reviews it has received from actual readers like you:

> "A little over 40 years ago, just before I turned 20, I went through a crisis of faith. I had been raised in a church, but was having doubts. I took a critical look at Christianity. I realized Christianity stood or fell on the central event of the faith, the resurrection of Jesus. I looked in a number of places and was able to find answers that convinced me the resurrection of Jesus was not just a statement of faith, but a verifiable event of history. It took a lot of searching and a few wrong turns for me to come to a satisfying conclusion. If I could, I would go back and give this book to my 19-year-old self. It addresses the questions I was asking then in a logical, coherent way. It is a short book, written in plain English. It is not heavy on theological terminology. It is ideal for the believer who needs reassurance as well as the unbeliever who wants to look at the central event of Christianity in a thoughtful, nonthreatening way." – Dana Roseman

"Dr. Morris has published an outstanding book on the death and resurrection of Jesus Christ. Not only is the information contained in his book a confirmation of the foundation of the Christian faith but it is also food for thought for all skeptics, critics, and doubters with respect to the divinity of Jesus. Dr. Morris has carefully and concisely presented historical information regarding both Scriptural and non-Scriptural evidence for the crucifixion, death, and resurrection of Jesus. I recommend this book to anyone who wants to gain a better understanding of these important historical events which have indeed had a lasting and profound impact on the history of all mankind." – Dennis Coleman

"This is an excellent book to give to a skeptic or unbeliever of any age. It plainly outlines the arguments for the Resurrection by engaging with some of the popular theories of what might have happened to Jesus' body. The book also includes clear historical evidence for the Resurrection from outside of the Bible as well as helpful and thought provoking questions at the end of each chapter for personal reflection or small group discussions. *Resurrected!* is an engaging, well written, plain talking book. It would make an excellent Easter gift for someone who is searching for the truth about Jesus." – Kim Sandy

"This book explains clearly and systematically historical proof of Christ's Lordship and leaves no doubt that He died and rose again. This short but very profound read is a must-help for Christians who believe but sometimes experience difficulty answering questions thrown their way. The reflection and study questions at the end of each chapter are insightful and enable one to think through and reflect on their relationship with Christ." – Pauline Yu Wikoff

"Are you a non-Christian who is curious about claims that Jesus was crucified and rose from the dead? Are you a Christian who is having doubts or just wondering what evidence there could possibly be? Are you fearful of death or what may happen to you in the future? I recommend this book to everyone! It covers all the points, and it has an excellent set of questions in each chapter that can be used for group study or for examining one's own beliefs. It is concise and explained well." – Marianne Leclerc

Now, in this Second Edition of *Resurrected!*, Dr. Morris gives us even more: more insight, more commentary, and more evidence from outside the Bible concerning the most important event in human history – and why it matters.

This book is dedicated to the Lamb of God, Jesus Christ, who died to take away our sins and then rose from the dead to prove that He is who and what He said He is:

> *Then the high priest stood up before the others and asked Jesus, "Well, aren't you going to answer these charges? What do you have to say for yourself?" But Jesus was silent and made no reply. Then the high priest asked him, "Are you the Messiah, the Son of the Blessed One?" Jesus said, "I am. And you will see the Son of Man seated in the place of power at God's right hand and coming on the clouds of heaven."*
>
> Mark 14:60–62, NLT

Contents

	Preface · xv
Chapter 1	What Is at Stake · · · · · · · · · · · · · · · · · 1
Chapter 2	Death on a Cross · · · · · · · · · · · · · · · · · 11
Chapter 3	Burial Tomb · 31
Chapter 4	Post-Resurrection Appearances · · · · · · · 41
Chapter 5	Transformed Lives · · · · · · · · · · · · · · · · 53
Chapter 6	Why It Matters to You · · · · · · · · · · · · · · 77
	Epilogue · 89
	Suggested Reading · · · · · · · · · · · · · · · · 97
	About the Author · · · · · · · · · · · · · · · · · 99
	Thank You · 101

Resurrected!

The Historical Truth
of the Most Important Event
in Human History -
And Why It Matters

(Second Edition)

Preface

Whenever I teach or lead a retreat as an evangelist, I try to give those attending something in writing that can further their journey of faith. Likewise, whenever I talk with those who want to know more about Jesus Christ or Christianity, I try to give them something in writing that they can read and think about. What I have found, however, is that there is a scarcity of written materials which are short enough to be readable in our busy world but long enough to be worth the reader's effort. The Word of God (the Bible) is always at the top of my list of suggested reading, but sometimes those with whom I am interacting do not have the time, interest, or ability to tackle this challenge, or they want something less formidable to begin – or continue – their journeys.

From my own experience with thousands of people, the ideal book for evangelism, that is, for sharing the Good News of Jesus Christ with others, should address an important topic of faith and be available to anyone who wants a copy. It should be clear and concise. It should provide references to source materials without becoming a textbook or treatise. It should be thought provoking and encourage further inquiry or discussion.

That is why I wrote this book.

I wrote *Resurrected!*, including the questions for personal reflection or small group discussion at the end of each chapter, as well as Chapter 6 in its entirety ("Why It Matters to You"), for the purpose of placing it in your hands so that you could, in turn, place it in the hands of others.

There are so many people in our world and in our lives who do not know Jesus Christ and have not experienced His love, compassion, and mercy. Some have never heard of Him. Others are aware of His name but have never discovered what is at the heart, and in the heart, of the man from Nazareth. Still others say they know Him because they are already Christians, but, when pressed to differentiate themselves from the world around them, they struggle to explain how their faith affects their lives or the lives of their loved ones on a daily basis.

Jesus proclaimed that He came into this world so that you could have life and have it abundantly (John 10:10). He wanted His joy to be in you and your joy to be complete (John 15:11). But none of this is possible unless – and until – you know who and what Jesus truly is.

What I am talking about does not require any formal training or theological study on your part. It is not premised on academic skills or the ability to memorize Bible verses. It is about having a loving relationship with the Creator of the universe through His Son, Jesus, who cared enough about you to die for you.

Because you are reading this book, one of two scenarios likely applies to you. Either you love someone enough to want them to know and experience Jesus as you do, or you are loved by someone who wants nothing less than that for you.

It is now in your hands – literally – to decide what to do with this book. I pray that each copy will awaken in the reader a new love for the Savior of the world and a deeper and more abiding belief in the event that changed history, and your eternal destiny, forever.

Dr. John Morris

CHAPTER 1
What Is at Stake

If you declare with your mouth, "Jesus is Lord," and believe in your heart that God raised him from the dead, you will be saved. For it is with your heart that you believe and are justified, and it is with your mouth that you profess your faith and are saved. As Scripture says, "Anyone who believes in him will never be put to shame." For there is no difference between Jew and Gentile – the same Lord is Lord of all and richly blesses all who call on him, for, "Everyone who calls on the name of the Lord will be saved."

Romans 10:9–13, NIV

DR. JOHN MORRIS

I once heard a pastor ask those who were gathered, "Jesus Christ rose from the dead. How do we know this to be true?"

Silence.

"It is an important event in our faith as Christians," he continued.

More silence.

"How do we know? How can we be sure?"

You could have heard the proverbial pin drop.

He then reached down, picked up his Bible, thrust it into the air, and declared, "Because the Bible tells us so!"

Many Christians accept the Bible as the inspired and inerrant Word of God. Historically accurate and theologically complete, Sacred Scripture is, for them, both the beginning and the end of their inquiry into the events described in the twenty-seven books comprising the New Testament, especially the events surrounding the life, death, and resurrection of Jesus of

Nazareth. Their mantra is simple but far-reaching: "For those who believe, no explanation is necessary. For those who do not believe, no explanation is possible."

There are, however, at least three major problems with this approach.

First, not everyone accepts the Bible as the inspired and inerrant Word of God – not even all Christians. For those who do not, inquiry and investigation are the keys to finding a faith worth living. Their mantra is equally simple and far-reaching: "A faith that has never been tested can never be trusted."

Second, Jesus told us to go into the world and preach the Good News – His life-changing and soul-saving story – "to everyone" (Mark 16:15, NLT). Furthermore, the Great Commission, which is understood by most Christians as applying to everyone who believes in Jesus, requires us to "go and make disciples of all the nations" (Matthew 28:19, NLT). However, we cannot do any of this if we remain in our spiritual bubbles while convincing ourselves that the Good News of Jesus Christ cannot be explained or verified as historically true to people who are not already Bible-believing Christians.

Third, many people are genuinely searching for joy and peace in their lives, and they want to know that whatever is offered as the answer to their quest will not collapse under its own weight when tragedy strikes or questions arise. For these individuals, both Christians and non-Christians alike, the Bible may be an important consideration, but they are unwilling to accept it automatically – some would say uncritically – as the foundation for their life's journey, especially if major changes to their current lifestyles may be required.

At the heart of all of this, and at the heart of the New Testament and Christianity itself, is Jesus of Nazareth.

Each year, typically in March or April, the mainstream media breaks out its many accounts of "The Real

Jesus." They challenge what we believe, cast doubt on everything from Jesus to the Bible itself, and, in the end, wish us a "Happy Easter" while leaving a path of theological destruction in their wake. Yes, we can ignore them, but what about those who don't – or can't? What about those who are seeking a better life in this world and an eternal union with God in the world to come? What about our own loved ones, especially our children and grandchildren, who, when they encounter spiritual battles, may begin to doubt, or even deny, everything they once believed and were taught?

Understanding our Christian faith, including the most important historical events upon which it is based, gives us additional spiritual ammunition in the fight for souls. I, for one, want to know and do everything I can to bring others to Christ, and doing so – in fact, my very faith as a Christian – hinges on the reality of the Resurrection. But don't take my word for that; instead, read what the Apostle Paul wrote to the community of believers in Corinth after his encounter with the Risen Christ almost two thousand years ago:

> But tell me this – since we preach that Christ rose from the dead, why are some of you saying there will be no resurrection of the dead? For if there is no resurrection of the dead, then Christ has not been raised either. And if Christ has not been raised, then all our preaching is useless, and your faith is useless. And we apostles would all be lying about God – for we have said that God raised Christ from the grave. But that can't be true if there is no resurrection of the dead. And if there is no resurrection of the dead, then Christ has not been raised. And if Christ has not been raised, then your faith is useless and you are still guilty of your sins. In that case, all who have died believing in Christ are lost! And if our hope in Christ is only for this life, we are more to be pitied than anyone in the world.
>
> 1 Corinthians 15:12–19, NLT

In this book, we will be using sources from outside the Bible, as well as our own critical thinking skills, to answer the following four questions:

- Did Jesus die on the cross?
- Was His tomb empty on the third day, and, if so, why?
- Did His followers see Him again after He was crucified and buried?
- Did He rise from the dead?

All I ask of you are two things.

First, set aside any biases or preconceptions you may have. Be open to all the possibilities.

Second, let the evidence be your guide. To paraphrase Socrates, "Follow the evidence, wherever it leads."

Questions for Personal Reflection or Small Group Discussion

1. As you begin reading this book, what do you believe about the resurrection of Jesus of Nazareth? Why?
2. If someone could prove to you that the Resurrection had never really happened, what would that do to your faith? What would it do to your belief in, or understanding of, the Bible?
3. If someone could prove to you that the Resurrection had actually occurred, what would that do to your faith? What would it do to your belief in, or understanding of, the Bible?
4. If a non-Christian came to you and, with all sincerity, asked you to tell him or her about Jesus, what would you say? Would you rely only on the contents of the Bible? What if the person were from a faith tradition that refused to accept our

Bible, especially the New Testament Gospels, as historically accurate?

5. If you or your loved ones were to encounter an event so unsettling that it called into question everything you or they believed about God, what would you do? Where would you go to find the supernatural strength to bring peace back into your hearts again?

6. During spiritual battle, if you could always come back to, and rely on, one indisputable fact, what would that be for you? What if the Resurrection, and everything it means and implies, could be that fact for you?

CHAPTER 2
Death on a Cross

Later, knowing that everything had now been finished, and so that Scripture would be fulfilled, Jesus said, "I am thirsty." A jar of wine vinegar was there, so they soaked a sponge in it, put the sponge on a stalk of the hyssop plant, and lifted it to Jesus' lips. When he had received the drink, Jesus said, "It is finished." With that, he bowed his head and gave up his spirit.

Now it was the day of Preparation, and the next day was to be a special Sabbath. Because the Jewish leaders did not want the bodies left on the crosses during the Sabbath, they asked Pilate to have the legs broken and the bodies taken down. The soldiers therefore came and broke the legs of the first man who had been crucified with Jesus, and then those of the other. But when they came to Jesus and found that he was already dead, they did not break his legs.

> Instead, one of the soldiers pierced Jesus' side with a spear, bringing a sudden flow of blood and water. The man who saw it has given testimony, and his testimony is true. He knows that he tells the truth, and he testifies so that you also may believe. These things happened so that the scripture would be fulfilled: "Not one of his bones will be broken," and, as another scripture says, "They will look on the one they have pierced."
>
> John 19:28–37, NIV

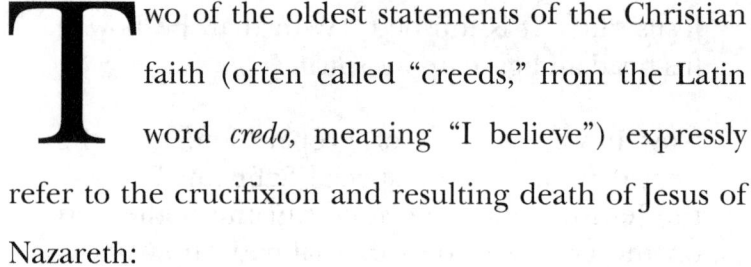

Two of the oldest statements of the Christian faith (often called "creeds," from the Latin word *credo*, meaning "I believe") expressly refer to the crucifixion and resulting death of Jesus of Nazareth:

- "I believe in ... one Lord Jesus Christ, the Only Begotten Son of God... For our sake he was

crucified under Pontius Pilate, he suffered death and was buried" (Nicene Creed, AD 325).
- "I believe in ... Jesus Christ, [the] only Son [of God] our Lord, who ... suffered under Pontius Pilate, was crucified, died, and was buried" (Apostles' Creed, AD pre-391).

These words are evidence of Christianity's belief, for more than sixteen hundred years (even longer, based on parts of more ancient texts), that Jesus died on the cross. However, they are not evidence of the event itself. All four of the Gospels (Matthew, Mark, Luke, and John) describe the actual events, but some nonbelievers, especially during the last two hundred years, have scoffed at these accounts, arguing that Jesus never really died on the cross – and perhaps was never even crucified. Let's examine this more closely.

Historical Evidence

Historical evidence of the death of Jesus on the cross is found in such ancient writings as *Jewish Antiquities*, which was written in AD 93–94 (about sixty years after the crucifixion of Jesus) by Flavius Josephus, a Jewish general who later became a respected historian for the Romans. In this documented account of the Jewish people, Josephus, who was not a Christian and never became a Christian, states the following about certain events that had occurred during his and his father's lifetimes:

> At this time [when Pontius Pilate was governor of Judea] there was a wise man called Jesus, and his conduct was good, and he was known to be virtuous. Many people among the Jews and the other nations became his disciples. *Pilate condemned him to be crucified and to die.* But those who had become his disciples did not abandon his discipleship. They reported that he had appeared to them three days *after his crucifixion* and that he was *alive*.[1]

---

[1] Paul L. Maier, translator/editor, *Josephus: The Essential Writings* (Grand Rapids, MI: Kregel, 1988), 264 (emphasis added).

From this written account by Josephus, it is clear that Jesus was condemned by Pilate to be crucified and to die, that He was crucified, and that He died on the cross.

Another ancient text, also written by a non-Christian, confirms that Jesus did in fact die on the cross.

Cornelius Tacitus, the Roman historian who wrote *Annals of Imperial Rome* in AD 109 (about seventy-five years after the crucifixion of Jesus), recorded the following in Book XV of his work:

> Nero fastened the guilt [for the fire that burned much of Rome in AD 64] and inflicted the most exquisite tortures on a class hated for their abominations, called Christians by the populace. *Christus, from whom the name had its origin, suffered the extreme penalty during the reign of Tiberius at the hands of one of our procurators, Pontius Pilatus,* and a most mischievous superstition, thus checked for the moment, again broke out not only in Judaea, the first source of the evil, but even in Rome, where all things hideous and shameful

from every part of the world find their centre and become popular.²

Here, the reference by Tacitus to "Christus" is clearly a reference to Jesus of Nazareth, who, in the Greek language, was called "Christ," meaning "Anointed One." Indeed, no other person in Roman history could be described as the "origin" from whom Christians took their name.³ And what ultimately happened to Jesus? According to Tacitus, He "suffered the extreme penalty during the reign of Tiberius at the hands of one of our procurators, Pontius Pilatus." Thus, as recorded by

---

2 Cornelius Tacitus, *Annals of Imperial Rome*, XV:44 (emphasis added), translated by Alfred John Church and William Jackson Brodribb, available online at the Internet Classics Archive (Massachusetts Institute of Technology), http://classics.mit.edu/Tacitus/annals.11.xv.html. In 1961, a two-foot by three-foot stone was discovered at Caesarea on which the name of Pontius Pilate, with his surname bearing the Roman spelling "Pilatus," had been inscribed. Paul L. Maier, translator/editor, *Eusebius–The Church History: A New Translation with Commentary* (Grand Rapids, MI: Kregel, 1999), 379.
3 Josephus likewise states that "the tribe of the Christians" was named after Jesus. Maier, *Josephus*, 264–65. According to the Christian writer Luke, it was at Antioch that the believers in Jesus were first called Christians (Acts 11:26).

Tacitus, Jesus was put to death under Pontius Pilate – just as Josephus recorded in *Jewish Antiquities*.[4]

Importantly, no one – neither the Romans nor any of the other groups that opposed the rise of Christianity during the first three hundred years after Jesus – ever claimed that Jesus did not die on the cross. Such an argument was first raised more than one thousand years later, long after everyone who had personal knowledge of the relevant events and personal contact with the eye-witnesses had died.

For those who have denied the historical reality of the Resurrection, some begin by challenging the death of Jesus on the cross. Among these, two primary arguments are made.

---

[4] Other sources from antiquity that are sometimes cited for their references to the death of Jesus include Mara bar Serapion, Lucian of Samosata, and the Babylonian (Jewish) Talmud. However, each of these has been questioned, and at times rejected, because of issues concerning the author, when the document was written, and whether the writing actually refers to Jesus of Nazareth. Thus, the works of Flavius Josephus and Cornelius Tacitus remain the strongest and most reliable sources from non-Christian history.

The Imposter Theory

The first theory advanced by some is that the man who died on the cross outside the walls of Jerusalem looked like Jesus but was not Jesus. They argue either that an innocent man was mistaken for Jesus during the rush of events or that the followers of Jesus conspired to find and offer up a Jesus look-alike.

Both of these claims suffer from the same defect.

During the ordeal that followed, which lasted hours, not minutes, the man who looked like Jesus would have undoubtedly protested or been recognized as being someone other than Jesus. First, he was arrested and taken before the Sanhedrin, the supreme Jewish court in Jerusalem. Then he was brought before Pontius Pilate, the Roman governor ("prefect") of Judea. After that, he was taken to Herod Antipas, who ruled Galilee by appointment from the Roman emperor. Then he was brought back to Pontius Pilate and presented to a frenzied crowd. After that, he was scourged and then forced to carry a cross one-third of a mile (a distance of more than five modern football fields) to a hill called Golgotha, where he was crucified. Despite all of this man's pain and suffering, and despite the length of time he spent with various people of diverse positions and allegiances, historical writings from the period make no mention of any protests from him concerning his identity, nor do they refer to any confusion about his identity while dealing with him.

In summary, the historical evidence as recorded by Josephus and Tacitus in antiquity, together with the absence of any evidence to the contrary, shows that the person nailed to the cross that day was Jesus of Nazareth.

The Swoon Theory

The second theory against Christianity's belief that Jesus died on the cross concedes that the victim was Jesus but argues that He was still alive when He was taken down from the cross. This so-called swoon theory relies on the incompetence of the Roman executioners that day or the existence of a conspiracy involving the family or followers of Jesus, and perhaps even the Romans, to ensure that Jesus would be taken down from the cross before He died.

First, as to the alleged incompetence of the Roman executioners, the fact is that although the Romans did not invent crucifixion, they perfected it as a form of torture and capital punishment that was designed to produce a slow death with maximum pain and suffering.[5] Furthermore, the main goal of crucifixion by the Romans was to instill terror – not in the victim but in the onlookers and general population of an area under Roman control. "Look upon this person," the Romans

---

[5] William D. Edwards, MD, Wesley J. Gabel, MDiv, and Floyd E. Hosmer, MS, AMI, "On the Physical Death of Jesus Christ," *Journal of the American Medical Association*, 255, No. 11 (March 21, 1986): 1455, 1458 (footnotes omitted).

were saying. "Don't give us any trouble. Don't let this happen to you." Such a diabolical objective, which was successful throughout the Roman Empire, would never have been possible unless Roman crucifixioners were able to perform their gruesome duty each time they were ordered to do so.

Second, as to a possible conspiracy involving the family or followers of Jesus that did not include the Romans, such a plan would have been virtually impossible to implement in order to ensure a staged but believable death of Jesus. Remember, this was almost two thousand years ago; technology was nonexistent, medicine was not well developed (and certainly not well applied in this part of the Roman Empire), and the variables for such a scam would have been far too numerous and complex to succeed. Also, the followers of Jesus – fishermen, a tax collector, and other "nobodies" from Galilee – were hardly the slick con men of their day. Even money could not have bought the necessary arrangements, unless the

DR. JOHN MORRIS

Romans were involved as well, because someone still had to put the entire plan together and then get away with it despite the watchful eyes of the Roman authorities and soldiers in and around Jerusalem.

But what if the Romans were part of the conspiracy?

If the conspirators included Roman soldiers, then they certainly had much to lose. Punishment was swift and severe for any Roman soldier who intentionally failed to perform his duty. For those tasked to crucify an enemy of Rome, the punishment would have been death, perhaps even death by crucifixion. The calculation of risk to reward would have been a chilling one in the case of Jesus or anyone else sentenced to be crucified.

What if someone as important as Pontius Pilate had been involved in the conspiracy? Some argue that in such a setting, the Roman soldiers and crucifixioners could have staged a believable death of Jesus without actually killing Him.

The medical facts surrounding the practice of crucifixion reveal the weakness of this argument as well:

> With knowledge of both anatomy and ancient crucifixion practices, one may reconstruct the probable medical aspects of this form of slow execution. ... With arms outstretched but not taut, the wrists were nailed to the patibulum [the horizontal crossbar]. Most commonly, the feet were fixed to the front of the stipes [the vertical post of the cross] by means of an iron spike... Although scourging may have resulted in considerable blood loss, crucifixion per se was a relatively bloodless procedure, since no major arteries, other than perhaps the deep plantar arch, pass through the favored anatomic sites of transfixion.
>
> The major pathophysiologic effect of crucifixion, beyond the excruciating pain, was a marked interference with normal respiration, particularly exhalation... The weight of the body, pulling down on the outstretched arms and shoulders, would tend to fix the intercostal muscles in an inhalation state and thereby hinder passive exhalation. ... Adequate exhalation required lifting the body by pushing up on the feet and by flexing the elbows and adducting the shoulders... However, this maneuver would place the entire weight of the

body on the tarsals and would produce searing pain. Furthermore, flexion of the elbows would cause rotation of the wrists about the iron nails and cause fiery pain along the damaged median nerves. Lifting of the body would also painfully scrape the scourged back against the rough wooden stipes. ... As a result, each respiratory effort would become agonizing and tiring and lead eventually to asphyxia.

The actual cause of death by crucifixion was multifactorial and varied somewhat with each case, but the two most prominent causes probably were hypovolemic shock and exhaustion asphyxia. Other possible contributing factors included dehydration, stress-induced arrhythmias, and congestive heart failure with the rapid accumulation of pericardial and perhaps pleural effusions. Crucifracture (breaking the legs below the knees), if performed, led to an asphyxic death within minutes. Death by crucifixion was, in every sense of the word, excruciating (Latin, *excruciatus*, or "out of the cross").[6]

Even if Pontius Pilate had been involved in a conspiracy to free Jesus by staging His death, the physiological

---

[6] Edwards et al., "On the Physical Death of Jesus Christ," 1455, 1460–61 (footnotes omitted).

effects of the act of crucifixion would have begun to take place once Jesus was nailed to the cross: dehydration, stress-induced arrhythmias, congestive heart failure, rapid accumulation of pericardial and perhaps pleural effusions, hypovolemic shock, and exhaustion asphyxia. Furthermore, in order to convince the Jewish leaders, other witnesses, and all of those not involved in the alleged conspiracy that Jesus was in fact dead, the Romans would have had to leave Him hanging from the cross for hours, not minutes, because a victim of crucifixion generally lasted three or four hours, to as much as three or four days, before dying.[7] Thus, the chances of Jesus escaping death were immeasurably small regardless of who was involved in any such conspiracy.

During one of my presentations on the Resurrection, a young man raised the possibility that Jesus was in a drug-induced coma, but not dead, when He was taken

---

[7] Edwards et al., "On the Physical Death of Jesus Christ," 1455, 1459–60 (footnotes omitted).

down from the cross. The young man even pointed out that, according to John's Gospel, Jesus received wine vinegar while He was hanging from the cross.[8] What if, as part of a conspiracy, the drink had been premixed with a drug that would have caused Jesus to appear to be dead although He was still alive? First, John's Gospel also records that a Roman soldier pierced the side of Jesus with a spear to ensure that He was dead before being taken down from the cross,[9] which was consistent with established crucifixion practices by the Romans at the time.[10] Second, the medical evidence quoted earlier demonstrates that if Jesus had been drugged in a way that made Him appear to be dead while hanging from the cross, then His body would have immediately ceased moving and slumped downward in the crucified position,

---

8 John 19:28–30.
9 John 19:31–37.
10 Edwards et al., "On the Physical Death of Jesus Christ," 1455, 1460 (footnotes omitted).

"thereby hinder[ing] passive exhalation," which, in turn, would have led "to an asphyxic death within minutes."[11]

To summarize, the swoon theory – whether based on an alleged conspiracy or the assumed incompetence of the Roman executioners – is contrary to the medical and historical realities of crucifixion practices in the ancient world and must therefore be rejected.

Following the Evidence, Wherever It Leads

If the imposter theory and the swoon theory cannot offer any credible alternatives to what Flavius Josephus and Cornelius Tacitus recorded in their non-Christian histories concerning the death of Jesus of Nazareth, then we must follow the evidence and conclude that when Jesus was taken down from the

---

[11] Edwards et al., "On the Physical Death of Jesus Christ," 1455, 1461 (footnotes omitted).

cross, He was in fact dead. Analyzing the historical and medical evidence, William Edwards, MD, writing in the *Journal of the American Medical Association*, agrees:

> It remains unsettled whether Jesus died of cardiac rupture or of cardiorespiratory failure. However, the important feature may be not *how* he died but rather *whether* he died. Clearly, the weight of historical and medical evidence indicates that Jesus was dead before the wound to his side was inflicted and supports the traditional view that the spear, thrust between his right ribs, probably perforated not only the right lung but also the pericardium and heart and thereby ensured his death... Accordingly, interpretations based on the assumption that Jesus did not die on the cross appear to be at odds with modern medical knowledge.[12]

---

12 Edwards et al., "On the Physical Death of Jesus Christ," 1455, 1463 (emphasis in original).

Questions for Personal Reflection or Small Group Discussion

1. If you were arguing that Jesus was not dead when the Roman soldiers took Him down from the cross, to what evidence would you point? Does it strike you as strange that the people who advance this theory have no such evidence?

2. What does it mean to you that none of the Romans, Jewish leaders, or other witnesses to the death of Jesus ever claimed that He was still alive when He was taken down from the cross? If someone were going to make such an argument, would you expect it to be someone – anyone – who had been present that day?

3. Christians believe that Jesus died to take away our sins and the sins of the entire world (see, for example, John 1:29, 3:16, 12:31–33; Mark 10:45; Matthew 20:28; Colossians 1:19–20; Ephesians

1:6–7). When you study the events of the day Jesus died, however, you come to realize how much He truly suffered. What does that say to you about how much He loves you?

4. If you had been at Golgotha the day Jesus was crucified, and if He had looked into your eyes from the cross, how would it have made you feel? Why?

5. If you could have spoken just a few words to Jesus that day, what would you have said to Him?

CHAPTER 3
Burial Tomb

Later, Joseph of Arimathea asked Pilate for the body of Jesus. Now Joseph was a disciple of Jesus, but secretly because he feared the Jewish leaders. With Pilate's permission, he came and took the body away. He was accompanied by Nicodemus, the man who earlier had visited Jesus at night. Nicodemus brought a mixture of myrrh and aloes, about seventy-five pounds. Taking Jesus' body, the two of them wrapped it, with the spices, in strips of linen. This was in accordance with Jewish burial customs. At the place where Jesus was crucified, there was a garden, and in the garden a new tomb, in which no one had ever been laid. Because it was the Jewish day of Preparation and since the tomb was nearby, they laid Jesus there.

John 19:38–42, NIV

As we saw in the previous chapter, two of the oldest statements of the Christian faith ("creeds") expressly refer to the crucifixion and resulting death of Jesus of Nazareth *as well as His burial:*

- "I believe in ... one Lord Jesus Christ, the Only Begotten Son of God... For our sake he was crucified under Pontius Pilate, he suffered death and was buried" (Nicene Creed, AD 325).
- "I believe in ... Jesus Christ, [the] only Son [of God] our Lord, who ... suffered under Pontius Pilate, was crucified, died, and was buried" (Apostles' Creed, AD pre-391).

In Chapter 2, we examined the question of whether Jesus died on the cross, and the evidence answered with a resounding yes. However, that does not conclude our inquiry into the Resurrection and the ultimate question of whether Jesus rose from the dead. We must next ask whether the tomb of Jesus was empty on the third day, and, if so, why?

For almost two thousand years, many nonbelievers have refused to accept Christianity's claim that Jesus of Nazareth rose from the dead after His crucifixion, death, and burial. Of the many arguments that have been made, none – until recently – ever challenged the fact that the tomb in which Jesus had been buried was empty on the third day when His followers began to report that He was alive.

The Wrong Tomb Theory

The modern-day argument that the tomb in which Jesus had been buried was not empty relies on the theory that, when the crucial time came to respond to the claim that Jesus had risen from the dead (a claim which arose only days and weeks after the death of Jesus), everyone – the Romans, the Jewish leaders, the followers of Jesus, the family of Jesus, and even the owner of the tomb (Joseph of Arimathea) – somehow forgot where the body of Jesus had been placed. As a result, or so the argument goes, they all looked in the wrong tomb – a tomb in which there was no body.

Of all the challenges to the Resurrection, this one fails to pass the "straight face" test.

When the time came to disprove the claims being made by the followers of Jesus that He had risen from the dead as He promised, the local authorities would have opened every tomb outside the gates of Jerusalem if doing so would have proven that Jesus was still there and still dead. They did not, however, because the location of the tomb of Jesus was known, and it was empty.

Then Where Did the Body Go?

Where did the body of Jesus go? Why was His tomb empty on the third day? There are several possible scenarios:

- The followers or family of Jesus, or others who were sympathetic to Him, stole His body.
- The Romans, the Jewish authorities, or others in collusion with one or both of these anti-Jesus groups stole His body.
- Grave robbers stole His body.
- Wild animals consumed His body.
- Jesus rose from the dead, just as His followers claimed and just as the Word of God says.

Upon further examination, some of these arguments lose their credibility almost immediately.

If the Romans, the Jewish authorities, or anyone acting on behalf of one or both of these groups had stolen the body of Jesus from the tomb, then they would have simply responded to the claim of Resurrection by producing His lifeless body for everyone to see. But this never happened.

The theory that grave robbers stole the body of Jesus from the tomb holds a certain superficial appeal, but any such bandits would have quickly discovered the futility of their crime (remember, these were Jewish tombs, not tombs of Egyptian pharaohs), and they would not have wasted further time or effort carrying away a body that offered them no financial gain or monetary benefit. Thus, the body of Jesus would have been discovered somewhere near the tomb, and that would have been the end of it. But this, too, never happened.

The argument that wild animals consumed the body of Jesus in the tomb was a gruesome possibility at the time, but there would have been clear evidence of this event at, in, and around the tomb. Furthermore, any such evidence would not have gone unnoticed by the Romans or the Jewish authorities in their ongoing opposition to Jesus and His followers. But, again, there was no such evidence.

We are therefore left with two factual alternatives. One appeals to human experience by concluding that the body of Jesus must have been stolen by His followers, His family, or others who were sympathetic to Him. The other appears to require a leap of faith by concluding that Jesus really did rise from the dead.

DR. JOHN MORRIS

Questions for Personal Reflection or Small Group Discussion

1. If you had to create a theory – any theory – to explain why the tomb of Jesus was empty when the matter came under investigation two thousand years ago, what would you suggest? Then, if you had to present evidence – any evidence – to support your theory, how would the lack of any such evidence affect it?
2. The empty tomb of Jesus of Nazareth is more than just one piece of the Resurrection puzzle; it is a crucial part of the events that Christians celebrate in the Risen Christ. Is there any part of your life that seems cold, dark, or lifeless like a tomb? What can you let the Risen Christ do to bring warmth, light, and life to that place?
3. Jesus called Himself "the way, the truth, and the life" (John 14:6, NLT). With regard to the empty

tomb, He is also "the way out." Is there anything in your life that needs the healing and forgiveness of our Heavenly Father? What are you willing to do to let Jesus lead you out of that situation once you are healed and forgiven?

4. Cemeteries, graves, and tombs often bring back memories of death and despair. The tomb of Jesus was like that once – for three days. Today, however, Christians should see His tomb as the staging area for every blessing ever accomplished in His name. Is there any area in your life that needs to be transformed from sadness into joy and from stillness into dancing? Do you believe that God, for whom all things are possible (Luke 18:27, Mark 10:27), can do that for you? What do you need to do to open the door of your life, and your heart, to Him (Revelation 3:20)?

CHAPTER 4
Post-Resurrection Appearances

On the evening of that first day of the week, when the disciples were together, with the doors locked for fear of the Jewish leaders, Jesus came and stood among them and said, "Peace be with you!" After he said this, he showed them his hands and side. The disciples were overjoyed when they saw the Lord. Again Jesus said, "Peace be with you! As the Father has sent me, I am sending you." And with that he breathed on them and said, "Receive the Holy Spirit."

John 20:19–22, NIV

In the preceding pages, we have tested the most common objections to Christianity's claim that Jesus of Nazareth rose from the dead after He was crucified.

In Chapter 2, we investigated the question of whether Jesus died on the cross. The evidence revealed that He did.

In Chapter 3, we studied the question of whether the tomb of Jesus was empty on the third day, and, if so, why. The evidence demonstrated that the tomb was empty and that there were two possible reasons for this: either the body of Jesus was stolen by His followers, His family, or others who were sympathetic to Him, or He really did rise from the dead.

Before addressing these two alternatives, we need to examine whether the followers of Jesus reported that He had appeared to them after His death on the cross, and, in doing so, we need to see whether there is anything outside the Bible, especially in non-Christian history, addressing the matter. In short, there is.

Evidence from Non-Christian History

In Chapter 2, we examined an ancient writing called *Jewish Antiquities* that was written more than nineteen hundred years ago (in AD 93–94, about sixty years after the crucifixion of Jesus) by the Roman historian Flavius Josephus, who, importantly, was not a Christian and never became one. In this detailed account of the Jewish people, Josephus continued to describe certain events that had occurred during his and his father's lifetimes:

> At this time [when Pontius Pilate was governor of Judea] there was a wise man called Jesus, and his conduct was good, and he was known to be virtuous. Many people among the Jews and the other nations became his disciples. Pilate condemned him to be crucified and to die. But those who had become his disciples did not abandon his discipleship. *They reported that he had appeared to them three days after his crucifixion and that he was alive.* Accordingly, he was perhaps the Messiah ["Anointed One"], concerning whom the prophets have reported wonders. And the tribe of the Christians, so named after him, has not disappeared to this day.[13]

---

13 Maier, *Josephus*, 264–65 (emphasis added).

Josephus had no reason to include myths, legends, or fairy tales in the historical work he was writing for the Romans. He certainly had no reason to say anything at all about Jesus that was not historically true and factually verifiable. Thus, we can say with certainty that the reports of the appearances of Jesus to His followers after His death and burial were part of the established history of the time.[14]

Eyewitness Accounts from the Word of God

When we began this journey together, I told you we would be using sources from outside the Bible to prove that Jesus rose from the dead. However, we can properly refer to the New Testament writings, especially the four

---

[14] The reference by the Roman historian Cornelius Tacitus in AD 109 to "a most mischievous superstition" of the early Christians (see Chapter 2) could likewise refer to their belief that Jesus was the Son of God and had risen from the dead. Tacitus, *Annals of Imperial Rome*, XV:44.

Gospels (Matthew, Mark, Luke, and John), as well as the Acts of the Apostles (also written by Luke) and the letters of Paul (who was executed for being a Christian about AD 65, some thirty to thirty-five years after the crucifixion of Jesus), to learn what the followers of Jesus said they had seen just days and weeks after He was crucified.

First, the appearances of Jesus to His followers after His death and burial, as recorded in the New Testament, are numerous, and they come to us through different authors writing at different times and in different locations. Among these are the appearances of Jesus, in a resurrected body, to the following people:

- A group of women, including Mary Magdalene, who were outside the tomb (Luke 24:1–10, John 20:1–2, 11–18);
- Ten of the original twelve disciples of Jesus, who were hiding behind locked doors (John 20:19–24);

- The same ten disciples, as well as Thomas, another member of the original twelve disciples of Jesus (John 20:25–29, Acts 1:1–3);
- Peter, Thomas, Nathanael, James, John, and two other disciples, who were fishing in the Sea of Galilee (John 21:1–14);
- Cleopas and another disciple, who were on their way to the village of Emmaus (Luke 24:13–31); and
- More than five hundred of His followers at one time, "most of whom are still alive" (1 Corinthians 15:3–6, NLT).

Second, the post-Resurrection accounts given by the followers of Jesus have a special air of credibility about them, because fictional writings would have undoubtedly portrayed the supporting eyewitnesses in a better and more positive way.

For example, the very first appearance of Jesus after He rose from the dead, according to the Christian writers, was to a group of women, including Mary Magdalene (Luke 24:1–10, John 20:11–18). However, women at that time and place were considered by the Jews as well as the Romans to be unimportant and unreliable, and they could not testify as witnesses at all. In addition, the first report of the resurrected Jesus to His disciples was made by this group of women, but the Gospel writer recorded that "the story sounded like nonsense to the men, so they didn't believe it" (Luke 24:1–11, NLT).

Likewise, another Gospel author reported that the first post-Resurrection appearance of Jesus to ten of the remaining members of His original twelve disciples occurred while these men were hiding "behind locked doors because they were afraid of the Jewish leaders" (John 20:19, NLT).

These detailed and highly unflattering accounts are hardly the type of stories that the followers of Jesus would have written about themselves if they were fabricating how, when, and where they had seen Jesus after He rose from the dead.

The Possibilities

Even without the ancient Christian and non Christian writings described above, there are only three possibilities as to whether the followers of Jesus saw Him again after He was crucified and buried, and, if so, what they saw (leaving aside the arguments that what they saw was just a hallucination or the result of mass hysteria, both of which fail to consider the multiple sightings of Jesus by multiple people in multiple locations and at multiple times following His crucifixion and burial).

The three possibilities, which will be discussed in greater detail in the next chapter, are shown in the following table:

	Did the followers of Jesus see Him again after He was crucified and buried?	At that time, what was Jesus's physical condition?
Possibility #1	**No**	**No one knew**
Possibility #2	**Yes**	**Dead, or severely injured**
Possibility #3	**Yes**	**Resurrected**

What, then, is the answer to this riddle of possibilities? What is the answer from the evidence?

DR. JOHN MORRIS

Questions for Personal Reflection or Small Group Discussion

1. If you were going to make up facts to support a new movement or agenda, whether political, religious, or otherwise, would you try to make those facts as positive as you could in order to attract others to your cause? How would you explain that the earliest Christian writers made themselves and other eyewitnesses to the Resurrection look suspicious, if not downright pitiful?

2. As to whether the followers of Jesus saw Him again after His crucifixion and burial, can you think of any possibilities or combination of possibilities other than the three set forth in the table at the end of Chapter 4?

3. If your investigation of the Resurrection came down to just a one-in-three chance of being right, would you be willing to alter your life or

your lifestyle in a major way, much less risk your life, based on that chance? Do you think that the early Christians would have been any different in evaluating the matter of the Resurrection? What were they risking by following Jesus? What are you risking today?

4. If Jesus had not risen from the dead, and thus if the Resurrection had never occurred, what would that have meant as far as His claim that He was the Son of God (Mark 14:60–62)? What would it have meant as far as His command to love and serve others rather than just living for yourself? Would Christianity even exist as a religion today?

CHAPTER 5
Transformed Lives

Then Peter stood up with the Eleven, raised his voice and addressed the crowd: "Fellow Jews and all of you who live in Jerusalem, let me explain this to you; listen carefully to what I say...

"Fellow Israelites, listen to this: Jesus of Nazareth was a man accredited by God to you by miracles, wonders and signs, which God did among you through him, as you yourselves know. This man was handed over to you by God's deliberate plan and foreknowledge; and you, with the help of wicked men, put him to death by nailing him to the cross. But God raised him from the dead, freeing him from the agony of death, because it was impossible for death to keep its hold on him...

"Fellow Israelites, I can tell you confidently that the patriarch David died and was buried, and his tomb is here to this day. But he was a prophet and knew that God had promised him on oath that he would place one of his descendants on his throne. Seeing what was to come, he spoke of the resurrection of the Messiah, that he was not abandoned to the realm of the dead, nor did his body see decay. God has raised this Jesus to life, and we are all witnesses of it. Exalted to the right hand of God, he has received from the Father the promised Holy Spirit and has poured out what you now see and hear…

"Therefore let all Israel be assured of this: God has made this Jesus, whom you crucified, both Lord and Messiah."

When the people heard this, they were cut to the heart and said to Peter and the other apostles, "Brothers, what shall we do?" Peter replied, "Repent and be baptized, every one of you, in the name of Jesus Christ for the forgiveness of your sins. And you will receive the gift of the Holy Spirit. The promise is for you and your children and for all who are far off – for all whom the Lord our God will call."

With many other words he warned them; and he pleaded with them, "Save yourselves from this corrupt generation." Those who accepted his message were baptized, and about three thousand were added to their number that day.

Acts 2:14–41, NIV

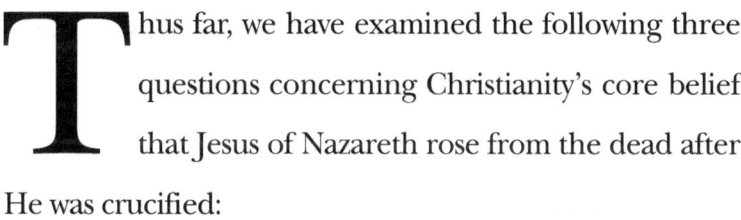

Thus far, we have examined the following three questions concerning Christianity's core belief that Jesus of Nazareth rose from the dead after He was crucified:

- Did Jesus die on the cross?
- Was His tomb empty on the third day, and, if so, why?
- Did His followers see Him again after He was crucified and buried?

Then, in the previous chapter, we identified three possibilities concerning the Resurrection itself:

- Possibility #1: The followers of Jesus never saw Him again after He was crucified and buried.
- Possibility #2: The followers of Jesus saw Him again after He was crucified and buried, but He was either dead or severely injured from His ordeal.
- Possibility #3: The followers of Jesus saw Him again after He was crucified and buried, and He was alive and well in a resurrected body that could pass through locked doors and appear or disappear at will.

Every possibility concerning Christianity's claim that, despite His crucifixion and burial, Jesus was alive and well in a resurrected body, can be found in one of these three alternatives. Furthermore, all remaining questions concerning whether Jesus died on the cross or whether His tomb was empty on the third day (and, if so, why) can be resolved once and for all based on these three possibilities.

Events Unfold in Jerusalem

After the crucifixion and burial of Jesus, His followers were in disarray. In fact, they had been in a state of confusion and panic from the time Jesus was first arrested at Gethsemane. According to Christianity's own written accounts, here is what happened:

- The followers of Jesus who were at Gethsemane with Him all ran when He was arrested (Matthew 26:36–38, 47–56; Mark 14:32–34, 43–52).
- Back in Jerusalem, Peter was identified as one of His followers, but Peter vehemently denied it three times (Matthew 26:69–75, Mark 14:66–72, Luke 22:54–62).

DR. JOHN MORRIS

- During and after the crucifixion of Jesus, His followers hid behind locked doors for fear that they, too, would be arrested and killed (John 20:19), while others simply left Jerusalem (Luke 24:13).

Thus, by the time the crucifixion and burial of Jesus had concluded, His followers were clearly – and understandably – afraid, confused, and disorganized. In the ordinary course of human events, their association with one another in the name of Jesus would have collapsed, and they would have been scattered (Acts 5:34–39).

Then came the reports that the followers of Jesus had seen Him again – not dead, nor severely injured from His ordeal (see Chapter 2 for the medical and physiological effects of crucifixion), but alive and well in a resurrected body (John 20:19–29, 21:1–14; Luke 24:13–31; Acts 1:1–3). Less than two months later, they were back on the streets of Jerusalem, healing others in the name of Jesus and boldly proclaiming that He was the Son of God and that He was alive (Acts 2:14–32, 3:1–16, 4:1–2, 4:8–10, 5:12–32).

What Was at Stake

Before examining what the followers of Jesus did after they allegedly saw Him alive and well in a resurrected body, it is crucial to analyze what they, or anyone else, would have known they were getting themselves into if they chose to proclaim that Jesus had risen from the dead and that He was the Son of God.

First, the followers of Jesus, all of whom were also Jews, already knew that He had been the target, and ultimately the victim, of the most powerful Jewish authorities in all the land. Now, as the purported witnesses to the Resurrection, His followers would be subject to the same scrutiny, and the same public humiliation, arrest, torture, and even death, if they chose to continue on the path Jesus had taken. On the other hand, if they slipped away from Jerusalem, returned to Galilee, and quietly took up their former occupations, they could enjoy long lives, families, safety, and security while living in obscurity.

Second, the Romans wanted no trouble in their provinces, and Judea was no exception. Although Pontius Pilate may not have cared whether Jesus lived or died, the Sanhedrin's concern with Jesus and His followers would, in time, spill over into confrontations with the Roman authorities as well. Furthermore, Rome itself would soon take an interest in the Christ controversy as the growth of Christianity began to have an impact on the Empire itself. Proclaiming the Resurrection as true and Jesus as the Son of God would place His followers in the crosshairs of the most powerful nation on earth.

Lastly, choosing to proclaim that Jesus had risen from the dead and was therefore the Son of God would have far-reaching social and religious consequences, including eternal consequences, for His followers. For example, declaring that Jesus was the Son of God would apparently require them to deny that there is only one God, Yahweh (Deuteronomy 6:4), and it would make them guilty of blasphemy – the same crime for which the Sanhedrin had convicted Jesus (Mark 14:53–64). In addition, proclaiming that Jesus had risen from the dead, if He did not, meant they would be lying about God, because they said that God raised Jesus from the dead (1 Corinthians 15:15). Thus, the best that the followers of Jesus could hope for on this path was ostracism from the Jewish community, while the worst – and more likely – outcome was arrest, torture, and death in this world and eternal damnation in the world to come.

What course of action would the followers of Jesus take? As both Jerusalem and Rome watched, they had to make a choice – and it all came down to the Resurrection.

The Rest of the Story

Despite receiving no earthly benefit or human reward for their efforts, and despite everything they knew would come against them, the closest followers of Jesus – formerly known as the Twelve and now known as the Apostles (by then Matthias had replaced Judas Iscariot, see Acts 1:12–26) – proclaimed the Risen Christ throughout the known world without any protest, disclaimer, or denial by any of them.

Here is what they received in return:[15]

- Peter, Andrew, Philip, Simon (also called the Zealot), and Jude (also known as Thaddaeus) were crucified.
- James, the son of Zebedee and brother of John, was beheaded.
- James, the son of Alphaeus, was beaten to death with a club.

---

15 Mark Water, compiler, *The New Encyclopedia of Christian Martyrs* (Grand Rapids, MI: John Hunt/Baker Books, 2001), 22–44.

- Matthew (also known as Levi) was beheaded.
- Bartholomew (also known as Nathanael) was "cruelly beaten" (some sources say flayed with a whip) and then crucified.
- Thomas (also known as Didymus) was killed with a spear.
- Matthias was stoned and then beheaded.
- John was boiled in oil (he did not die), then exiled to the mines of Patmos (he still did not die), and finally passed away in old age (the only one of the Twelve to do so), thereby serving as the living bridge from Jesus to the young church of the First Century.

What caused this transformation? What gave these men the courage, strength, and devotion to accept such hard and tragic lives when they could have easily avoided it all by renouncing Jesus and denying the Resurrection? The answer provides the key to unlocking the ultimate question of whether Jesus of Nazareth rose from the dead.

Here is where we left off at the end of Chapter 4:

	Did the followers of Jesus see Him again after He was crucified and buried?	At that time, what was Jesus's physical condition?
Possibility #1	**No**	**No one knew**
Possibility #2	**Yes**	**Dead, or severely injured**
Possibility #3	**Yes**	**Resurrected**

Possibility #1

If the followers of Jesus never saw Him again after He was crucified and buried, including if everyone was looking in the wrong tomb (discussed in Chapter 3), then it would have meant that His followers never saw Him in a resurrected body. As a result, they, like anyone else, would have had serious doubts about His claim that He was the Son of God. Furthermore, they, like anyone else, would have eventually concluded that what Jesus had prophesied – being handed over to the Jewish and Roman authorities, dying, and then rising from the dead on the third day (Matthew 20:17–19, Luke 24:7–8) – was simply not true. Thus, regardless of His physical condition, where He was, or how He got there, Jesus was apparently neither who nor what He had claimed to be.

Under this scenario, the followers of Jesus would have had no reason – not guilt, not sympathy, and not some sense of friendship, camaraderie, or adventure – for risking their lives for Him in Jerusalem or anywhere else. Possibility #1 must therefore be eliminated.

Possibility #2

If the followers of Jesus did see Him again after He was crucified and buried, but all they ever saw was His lifeless body, then it would have confirmed the theory (also discussed in Chapter 3) that they, the family of Jesus, or others sympathetic to Him had stolen His body from the tomb. More importantly, however, it would have meant that the followers of Jesus knew He had never risen from the dead.[16]

If the followers of Jesus did see Him again after He was crucified and buried, and He was alive although severely injured from His ordeal, then it would have confirmed the swoon theory (discussed in Chapter 2) that Jesus did not die on the cross. Again, however, it would have also meant that His followers knew beyond any doubt Jesus had never risen from the dead.[17]

---

[16] Some have speculated that what the followers of Jesus actually saw was His ghost. However, and leaving aside the threshold question of whether such apparitions even exist, people at the time of Jesus understood that a ghost was the disembodied spirit of someone who had died. See, for example, Henry Barclay Swete, *Commentary on Mark* (Grand Rapids, MI: Kregel, 1977), 138. Thus, if what the followers of Jesus saw was His ghost, then it would have again meant that they knew Jesus was dead and therefore had not been resurrected as He claimed He would be.

[17] If Jesus was never crucified at all, as argued by advocates of the imposter theory (also discussed in Chapter 2), then His followers, upon learning this fact, would have once again known for sure that Jesus had never risen from the dead.

Under any of these scenarios, the followers of Jesus would have known with absolute certainty that He was neither who nor what He had claimed to be.

Even the most loyal of associates would not have risked everything to proclaim that Jesus was the Son of God if they knew He was not. Likewise, even the most ardent of supporters would not have suffered for the privilege of pretending that Jesus had risen from the dead if they knew He had not. However, despite imprisonment, torture, and even death, the followers of Jesus never recanted their accounts of what they had seen. Possibility #2 must therefore be eliminated as well.

Possibility #3

Through the process of elimination, we are left with Possibility #3: the followers of Jesus saw Him again after He was crucified and buried, and He was alive and well in a resurrected body.

But is it enough to arrive at this conclusion simply through the process of elimination, especially when the conclusion will have so many far-reaching implications for our lives and the lives of our loved ones?

No, let's go further and test Possibility #3 against the evidence.

First, does Possibility #3, that is, the resurrection of Jesus of Nazareth really happened, account for the overwhelming medical and historical evidence that He died on the cross?

Check.

Second, does it establish why His tomb was empty on the third day?

Check.

Third, is it consistent with the historical record that His followers reported they saw Him again after He was crucified and buried?

Check.

Lastly, does it explain why His followers were willing to accept, and did in fact accept, the hard and tragic lives they endured for decades, as also recorded outside the Bible, when they could have easily avoided it all by renouncing Jesus and denying the Resurrection?

Check.

Thus, Possibility #3 – that the resurrection of Jesus of Nazareth really happened – is not only the one remaining possibility, but it is also the only possibility which accounts for, and is consistent with, the medical and historical evidence we have examined in this book.

If we are to follow the evidence wherever it leads, then Jesus of Nazareth did rise from the dead on that first Easter morning.

―――∞―――

During the early years of Christianity, some men began moving to the desert in an effort to pursue their spiritual journeys without the distractions of the world around them. Living in isolation and with none of the comforts otherwise found in society, they focused on Jesus Christ through prayer and self-denial. Such a life was hard, both physically and mentally, and few of those who tried this lifestyle were able to persevere.

One young man came to the desert, tried his best, but eventually decided to leave. Before returning to his village, he encountered a much older man who had not only survived the desert but also flourished there in his journey with Jesus. Wanting to discover why this elderly man had succeeded where so many others had failed, the young man asked him for the secret of his success.

"There is no secret," the old man said. "Many have tried, but only a few have stayed."

"But why?" the young man asked. "Why were you able to succeed?"

At that moment, the old man's dog, which had been sitting quietly at its master's feet, sprang up, cocked

RESURRECTED!

its ears, tilted its head, and raced away. The two men watched as the dog dashed toward a small clump of desert grass, from which popped a rabbit.

As the rabbit sped off, the old man's dog followed in hot pursuit, barking wildly but always keeping its eyes on the rabbit.

During the next few minutes, several other dogs joined the chase. Some were younger and faster than the old man's dog, but they soon comprised a single pack of canines, sprinting and yelping in the desert sun.

After a few more minutes, the dogs that had joined the chase began to drop out. One by one, the pack diminished until there was only one dog left – the old man's dog.

Nodding his head approvingly, the old man looked at his young companion and, with a gleam in his eyes, told him, "There is your answer."

The young man's face clearly showed his confusion.

DR. JOHN MORRIS

Catching a final glimpse of the old man's dog as the pursuer and its objective ran from sight, the young man turned back to his elder and managed only a few last words: "I…don't…understand."

Slowly the old man explained, "The other dogs heard my dog and saw him running, so they joined the hunt. However, the others eventually lost interest and went their own ways. Only one dog, my dog, continued the chase – because he had seen the rabbit."

"My young friend," the old man concluded, "whatever I may have accomplished in my pursuit of Jesus Christ, it is because I, too, have seen the rabbit."

Almost two thousand years ago, twelve men from Galilee gave up everything, including their lives, so that they could share with others the truth of the most important event in human history: the resurrection of Jesus of Nazareth from the dead. They did so, not because they had been His friends or because they had nothing else to do, but because they had all seen the Risen Christ – the Lamb of God – the Savior of the world.

That which was from the beginning, which we have heard, which we have seen with our eyes, which we have looked at and our hands have touched – this we proclaim concerning the Word of life. The life appeared; we have seen it and testify to it, and we proclaim to you the eternal life, which was with the Father and has appeared to us. We proclaim to you what we have seen and heard, so that you also may have fellowship with us. And our fellowship is with the Father and with his Son, Jesus Christ. We write this to make our joy complete.

1 John 1:1–4, NIV

DR. JOHN MORRIS

Questions for Personal Reflection or Small Group Discussion

1. If you had to explain why each and every one of the Apostles willingly accepted suffering and death for the sake of Jesus, do you think that loyalty to a lost cause would have been sufficient? Would their prior friendship with Jesus have been enough if they knew for certain that He was not who or what He had claimed to be?

2. One of the strongest human instincts is self-preservation. Thus, when faced with pain and death, even the toughest people will often say or do whatever is necessary to survive. But the Apostles didn't. Why?

3. Someone might try to explain the actions of the Apostles after the crucifixion and burial of Jesus by saying they were all crazy. But what evidence

of this is there? Furthermore, would the Roman Empire have worked so hard for so long (more than two hundred and fifty years) to silence a fringe group of lunatics that posed no physical or political danger? And if the Apostles were insane, how could they have convinced so many people that the Resurrection did occur and that Jesus was the Son of God – especially when accepting their stories meant imprisonment, torture, and often death for the new believers as well?

4. Of all the consequences awaiting the Apostles if they falsely proclaimed that Jesus was the Son of God and that He had risen from the dead, which one is most frightening to you? Ostracism? Arrest? Imprisonment? Torture? Death? Eternal damnation? Did any of these seem to matter to the Apostles, who claimed to have seen a resurrected Jesus? Why not?

5. People are sometimes willing to die for their subjective beliefs, but the Apostles were willing to die for an objective event: the Resurrection. Why would they all, without exception, have gone so willingly to their deaths if they knew that the Resurrection had never occurred?

CHAPTER 6
Why It Matters to You

> Jesus answered, "I am the way and the truth and the life. No one comes to the Father except through me."
>
> John 14:6, NIV

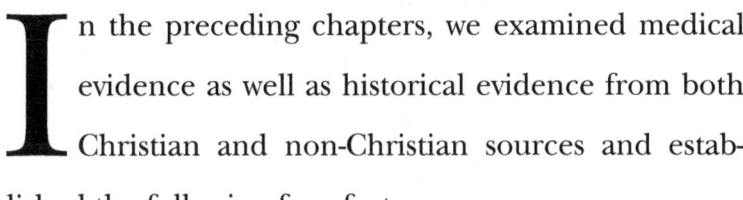

In the preceding chapters, we examined medical evidence as well as historical evidence from both Christian and non-Christian sources and established the following four facts:

- Jesus of Nazareth died on the cross.
- His tomb was empty on the third day.

- He rose from the dead.
- He appeared to His followers after the Resurrection.

All of this is important to our faith as Christians, but what practical difference does it make – can it make – in your individual life and in the lives of your loved ones today?

This final chapter is not an ending to the story of the Resurrection but a beginning to your story. Because Jesus did rise from the dead, there are ten specific truths on which you can bet your life – and your soul.

Truth #1: God Is Real

Man did not raise Jesus from the dead; God did. No science, medicine, or other human effort has ever, or will ever, return a dead body to a permanent state of life. (In this regard, you need to distinguish between "reanimation" and "resurrection," because every person who has ever been reanimated, that is, returned to a state of life after being clinically dead, eventually dies again, but once a person's body is resurrected, he or she is alive forever.) When atheists tell you that God is a myth or just a fairy tale, you know better, because Jesus was raised from the dead, and no one could do that except God. Oh, and when they tell you, "God is dead," you can look them in the eyes and say, "No, but His Son was dead once – and now He is alive forever!"

Truth #2: God Loves You More Than You Can Imagine

Sadly, there are those who believe in God but have never experienced His love. Although God is just, He is also merciful – and He loves you so much that He allowed His Son to become a man and then die for you in order to take away your sins and the sins of the entire world (see, for example, John 1:29, 3:16, 12:31–33; Mark 10:45; Matthew 20:28; Colossians 1:19–20; Ephesians 1:6–7). The Resurrection reveals the truth about the life and death of your Savior and how much God truly loves you.

Truth #3: Jesus Is the Son of God

During His trial before the Sanhedrin, Jesus was asked by the high priest, "Are you the Messiah, the Son of the Blessed One [in other words, the Son of God]?" Jesus answered, "I am. And you will see the Son of Man [Jesus' preferred way of referring to Himself, as originally described in Daniel 7:13–14] seated in the place of power at God's right hand and coming on the clouds of heaven" (Mark 14:60–62, NLT). Although you, too, are a child of God (John 1:12), there is only one eternally begotten Son of God (John 1:1), His name is Jesus, and God raised Him from the dead.

Truth #4: Heaven Is Real, and It Is Worth Living For

During His final meal with His followers before He was arrested and crucified (often called the Last Supper), Jesus told His followers that His Father's house – Heaven – has many rooms, and that He was going there to prepare a place for them and for you (John 14:2). God's supernatural act of raising Jesus from the dead was divine approval of the words Jesus spoke. The Apostle Paul tried to give you a glimpse of Heaven when he wrote, "No eye has seen, no ear has heard, and no mind has imagined what God has prepared for those who love him" (1 Corinthians 2:9, NLT). Heaven is real, and it is worth doing everything you can to get there and, in time, to bring your loved ones with you.

Truth #5: You Can Be Saved, and Your Loved Ones Can Be Saved As Well

In his Letter to the Ephesians, Paul stated that you are saved by grace, through faith (Ephesians 2:8). However, in his Letter to the Romans, he was even more specific on this point: "If you openly declare that Jesus is Lord and believe in your heart that God raised him from the dead, you will be saved" (Romans 10:9, NLT). The Resurrection gives you confidence to do both: Jesus is Lord, and God the Father did raise Him from the dead.

Truth #6: The Word of God Comes from God

In his Second Letter to his friend Timothy, Paul wrote that all of Scripture – the Word of God – is "inspired by

God" ("God-breathed"), it "is useful to teach us what is true and to make us realize what is wrong in our lives," it "corrects us when we are wrong and teaches us to do what is right," and "God uses it to prepare and equip his people to do every good work" (2 Timothy 3:16–17, NLT). The Resurrection proves that when you hold the Word of God in your hands, and when you share it with your loved ones, you are truly reading, speaking, and sharing the heart of God.

Truth #7: The Holy Spirit Will Teach You All Things and Guide You to All Truth

At the Last Supper, Jesus also promised that, after His resurrection, the Holy Spirit would come to teach you all things and guide you to all truth (John 14:26, 16:13). Within the church, the community of Christian believers that Paul called "the pillar and foundation of the truth" (1 Timothy 3:15, NLT), the Holy Spirit makes sure you can know and live the will of God. By the way, Jesus also promised that the gates of Hell itself would not prevail against those who believe in Him (Matthew 16:18), which is another promise confirmed by the Resurrection.

Truth #8: If You Return to God, He Will Return to You

America lost its way as a nation when it turned its back on God. Removing prayer from schools and public gatherings, thinking this country can be self-sufficient without God, and believing there are no objective moral truths have combined to make the United States a "weak reed, swayed by every breath of wind" (Matthew 11:7, NLT). However, God has promised, "Then if my people who are called by my name will humble themselves and pray and seek my face and turn from their wicked ways, I will hear from heaven and will forgive their sins and restore their land" (2 Chronicles 7:14, NLT). Because the Resurrection demonstrates that God does exist and that you can be reconciled with Him through Jesus, there is still hope for you and for America (Joel 2:12, Acts 3:19, 1 John 1:9).

Truth #9: Jesus Has Overcome the World, and So Can You

As Jesus talked about His impending suffering and death, He said to His followers, "I have told you all this so that you may have peace in me. Here on earth you will have many trials and sorrows. But take heart, because I have overcome the world" (John 16:33, NLT). The Resurrection attests that God, not man, has the final word; that you, like the followers of Jesus who witnessed Him as the Risen Christ, can endure, and in the end overcome, everything the world throws at you; and that, like those followers of Jesus, you can – and will – have ultimate victory through Him.

Truth #10: God Alone Can Give You Peace That Surpasses All Understanding

Every human heart longs for "God's peace, which exceeds anything we can understand" (Philippians 4:7, NLT). The Resurrection and the events that followed show us that true peace does not come from human power or earthly authority but from the throne of God. Thus, your lifelong goal, your guiding star above all other things, should be to reach Heaven at the end of your life and, in time, to bring as many others with you as possible – starting with your loved ones.

Jesus did His part.

His followers did their part.

Now it's up to us – you and me – to do ours.

Questions for Personal Reflection or Small Group Discussion

1. The ten truths described in this chapter are all found in the Word of God, on which God placed His seal of approval in the form of the Resurrection. Which of the ten mean the most to you? Why?
2. There are many other truths, and many other promises, contained in the Word of God, and the Resurrection confirms them all. Which ones are familiar to you, and, of them, which mean the most to you in your daily walk with Christ? Why?
3. In this final chapter, Dr. Morris stated that his words are not an ending to the story of the Resurrection but a beginning to your story. Do you believe this? What eternal impact can you have on the lives of others, especially your loved ones?

4. In the first reflection question in this book (Chapter 1), Dr. Morris asked what you believed about the resurrection of Jesus of Nazareth. Now that you have arrived at the conclusion of the book, how, if at all, have your beliefs about the Resurrection changed or become stronger?
5. For you personally, what is the most important message from the Resurrection? Why?

Epilogue

The effect of the Resurrection on our lives today cannot be overstated. It forms the very heart of our faith as Christians, equips us with courage and strength to address the most difficult situations in our lives, and empowers us with unwavering hope even when facing death itself.

Without the Resurrection, we would have none of these, and, as Paul the Apostle wrote so very long ago, we would be "more to be pitied than anyone in the world" (1 Corinthians 15:19, NLT).

DR. JOHN MORRIS

But we were not placed on this earth to be pitied. As Christians, we are called to be salt and light to a world still desperately in need of its Savior (Matthew 5:13–16).

Several years ago, I was asked to visit the home of a man who was dying. He was there with his family, and his wife and daughter confided in me that the man was fighting more than just his cancer – he was struggling with his faith. He had been a Christian his entire life, but, at what appeared to be his life's end, he was laboring to make sense of anything at all.

As I sat down and began to talk with him, our conversation quickly turned to God. Why was this happening to him? Where was the miracle for which he and his family had prayed? Was there life after death?

I have been asked these same questions many times in my ministry. They are valid questions – good questions – for anyone to ask when life is threatened or death is near.

Although there are many questions that will never be answered on this side of Heaven, God does provide answers – and more often than most people realize. Trite phrases, such as "God's ways are beyond our understanding" or "God must have needed another angel," are of no help at times such as these. Instead, knowing our Christian faith, including the most important historical events upon which it is based, is the key to having peace – and sharing peace – even in the face of death.

For the next hour, the man and I talked about Heaven, Jesus, and what he had believed since he was a boy. And, for the longest part of our conversation, we talked about the Resurrection.

Using some of the same truths I shared with you in the previous chapter, I quietly reassured the man that Heaven was real, God loved him, and Jesus was waiting for him on the other shore. He asked some final questions, and I offered my thoughts. We prayed. Then we prayed with his entire family. And I departed.

A few weeks later, the man's daughter called me to say that her father had died. She quickly added, however, that he had died in peace. After my visit, she said, his fears and spiritual struggles seemed to disappear, and, in the end, his faith was as strong as it had ever been.

Jesus died on the cross to give us eternal life, and He rose from the dead to give us living hope:

> Praise be to the God and Father of our Lord Jesus Christ! In his great mercy he has given us new birth into a living hope through the resurrection of Jesus Christ from the dead, and into an inheritance that can never perish, spoil or fade.
>
> 1 Peter 1:3–4, NIV

If you have never listened to the beautiful hymn "Because He Lives (Amen)" by Matt Maher, please give it a try. Here are the words (reprinted with permission),[18] which underscore the importance of the Resurrection to us today:

> I believe in the Son
> I believe in the Risen One
> I believe I overcome
> By the power of His blood
>
> Amen
> Amen
> I'm alive
> I'm alive
> Because He lives
> Amen
> Amen
> Let my song join the one that never ends
> Because He lives
>
> I was dead in the grave
> I was covered in sin and shame

---

18 "Because He Lives (Amen)," performed by Matt Maher, written by Ed Cash, Bill Gaither, Gloria Gaither, Matt Maher, Jason Ingram, Daniel Carson, and Chris Tomlin, © 2014 Hanna Street Music (BMI) / Sony/ATV Tree Publishing / I Am A Pilgrim Songs (BMI) / Sony/ATV Timber Publishing / Open Hands Music (SESAC) / Alletrop Music (BMI) / worshiptogether.com songs / sixsteps music (ASCAP) / Worship Together Music / sixsteps songs / SDG Publishing (BMI). Used by permission. All rights reserved.

DR. JOHN MORRIS

I heard Mercy call my name
He rolled the stone away

Amen
Amen
I'm alive
I'm alive
Because He lives
Amen
Amen
Let my song join the one that never ends

Because He lives
I can face tomorrow
Because He lives
Every fear is gone
I know He holds my life, my future in His hands

Amen
Amen
I'm alive
I'm alive
Because He lives
Amen
Amen
Let my song join the one that never ends

Amen
Amen
I'm alive

RESURRECTED!

> I'm alive
> Because He lives
> Amen
> Amen
> Let my song join the one that never ends
>
> Because He lives
> Because He lives

May the Risen Christ be with you always, and may He bless you and all of your loved ones as you continue your journey of faith with Him.

He is risen! He is risen indeed!

> Jesus said to her, "I am the resurrection and the life. The one who believes in me will live, even though they die; and whoever lives by believing in me will never die."
> John 11:25–26, NIV

Suggested Reading

As you continue your journey of faith, you may be interested in reading more about the Crucifixion and Resurrection. Here are some of my favorites:

1. Bishop, Jim. *The Day Christ Died.* New York: HarperOne/HarperCollins, 1991.
2. Habermas, Gary R., Antony Flew, and David J. Baggett. *Did the Resurrection Happen? A Conversation with Gary Habermas and Antony Flew.* Downers Grove, IL: InterVarsity Press, 2009.

3. Jeffrey, Grant R. *Jesus: The Great Debate.* Toronto: Frontier Research, 1999.
4. Lavoie, Gilbert R. *Resurrected: Tangible Evidence That Jesus Rose from the Dead* [Shroud of Turin]. Allen, TX: Thomas More, 2000.
5. Lucado, Max. *And the Angels Were Silent.* Nashville: W Publishing Group, 1987.
6. Lucado, Max. *Six Hours One Friday.* Nashville: W Publishing Group, 2004.
7. Strobel, Lee. *The Case for Christ.* Grand Rapids, MI: Zondervan, 1998.

About the Author

Dr. John Morris is a Christian author, speaker, and evangelist preaching the Gospel (Good News) of Jesus Christ. Ordained as a minister in 2002, he has bachelor's degrees in pastoral ministry and philosophy as well as a juris doctorate in law.

In his twenty-five years of ministry, Dr. Morris has served as an evangelist, worship pastor, spiritual director, Christian counselor, instructor of religious education, and deacon. In addition, he has spoken at statewide and national Christian conferences, given retreats on discipleship, spirituality, and evangelism, and been a

DR. JOHN MORRIS

guest presenter to both adults and youth groups at various churches.

Dr. Morris and his wife, Anne, have been married for thirty-five years. They have five children and four grandchildren.

If you would like to contact Dr. Morris or learn more about his ministry, visit his website at www.YourGreatGrace.net, including his blog "Finding Joy – Finding Peace – Finding Christ." He would love to hear from you.

Dr. Morris is also available on Facebook at www.facebook.com/YourGreatGrace and on Twitter at www.twitter.com/_YourGreatGrace.

Thank You

Thank you for taking the time to read *Resurrected! The Historical Truth of the Most Important Event in Human History–And Why It Matters*. If you enjoyed it, please consider posting a short review on Amazon.com (word of mouth is an author's best friend and much appreciated), and, in the spirit of evangelism, sharing your copy with someone you care about.

Thank you again, and I pray that God blesses you and your loved ones abundantly!

Dr. John Morris

CPSIA information can be obtained
at www.ICGtesting.com
Printed in the USA
BVHW042004210621
610146BV00015B/663